Deer, Elk & Moose

GRAND AND MAJESTIC CREATURES

BY STAN TEKIELA

Adventure Publications, Inc.
Cambridge, MN

DEDICATION

This book is dedicated to the field naturalists who have dedicated their lives to environmental education. All of your work makes a difference.

ACKNOWLEDGMENTS

The following people and organizations have been instrumental in obtaining some of the images in this book. For all that you do, thank you.

Agnieszka Bacal • Michael Bertelsen • Ron Green • Lee Greenly, Minnesota Wildlife Connection (Sandstone) • Barrett Hedges • Mammal Collection, Bell Museum of Natural History, University of Minnesota (St. Paul)

Special thanks to Rick Bowers, wildlife biologist and extraordinary friend, for reviewing this book. I am continually impressed and amazed at your in-depth knowledge of wildlife.

Cover photos by Stan Tekiela
All photos are by Stan Tekiela except the following: pg. 19 by Mel Diotte, Windsor, Ontario, Canada (piebald); pg. 19 by Jerry Stone (black); pp. 74–75 and pg. 86 by Michael H. Francis; pg. 76 from Shutterstock; pg. 77, "Elk Tracks" by Katie Theule/USFWS licensed according to a Creative Commons 2.0 Attribution license (https://creativecommons.org/licenses/by/2.0/), original available at www.flickr.com/photos/usfwsmtn-prairie/14730606803; pg. 134 by Rick and Nora Bowers. Some photos were taken under controlled conditions.

Edited by Sandy Livoti
Cover and book design by Jonathan Norberg

Copyright 2015 by Stan Tekiela
Published by Adventure Publications, Inc.
820 Cleveland Street South
Cambridge, MN 55008
1-800-678-7006
www.adventurepublications.net
ISBN: 978-1-59193-459-2

TABLE OF CONTENTS

When I think of wildlife, deer and creatures like them come to mind. White-tailed Deer, exquisite animals with soulful eyes, are found in nearly every habitat and clime. In the mountains on a frosty autumn morning, it's exciting to see a male elk puffing steam as he bugles to his harem of cows. Moose, huge creatures of the boreal forest, are gentle souls with easygoing personalities. I am always struck by the calm, reassuring nature of these sentinels of the Northwoods.

I have spent the last 30 years traveling, studying and photographing mammals. From the Florida Keys to Maine's rocky coast, across the northland to the Rockies and into the Alaskan wilderness, you won't find a more interesting group of animals than deer, elk and moose. It is my pleasure to present their lives and behaviors, complemented with images that capture their majesty and beauty. I hope you'll enjoy this photographic adventure and celebrate these wonderful animals with me.

White-tailed Deer

Elk

Moose

Moose

The ancestors of our White-tailed Deer first appeared in South and Central America 40–50 million years ago. The species as we know it today expanded northward, inhabiting nearly all of North America. Whitetails are still continuing to move north, into the Canadian Yukon.

The first elk-like animals lived in Eurasia 25 million years ago. They didn't appear in North America until much later, 10–15 million years ago. For centuries it was thought that our North American elk were a subspecies of the smaller European Red Deer, but scientists determined in 2004 that they are a distinct species unique to the Americas.

Moose may have evolved on the European continent 500,000 years ago, arriving in North America much more recently, at the same time as elk. Today moose are found in northern latitudes around the world where there is suitable habitat, such as near Mount McKinley in Denali National Park, Alaska, as shown.

White-tailed Deer

THE DEER FAMILY

The deer family, or Cervidae, in North America includes White-tailed Deer, Mule Deer, elk, moose and caribou. These closely related animals are classified in the order Artiodactyla, which means "even-toed" and refers to their even number of toes on each foot. From Artiodactyla, they are categorized into the Ruminantia suborder. This class includes ruminants—animals with more than one stomach, enabling them to regurgitate food and chew it again, or chew the cud.

The White-tailed Deer, often just called Whitetail, was named for the large patch of white fur under its tail. When the scientific name *Odocoileus virginianus* was assigned in 1832, it was actually a mistake. The genus name *Odocoileus* was based on a hollow tooth found in the fossilized remains of a deer, but it should have been called *Odontocoileus*, with *Odonto* referring to the tooth. This was never changed due to the tendency to keep the honor of original names. The species *virginianus* refers to the large territory of Virginia, indicating a widespread southern range.

White-tailed Deer

Elk are also known as Wapiti, which comes from Shawnee and Cree Indian words that translate to "white rump" or "pale deer." This accurately describes the backside of an elk when it runs away. The genus *Cervus* groups our North American elk, most of the large deer-like animals in Eurasia and one species in Africa. The species *canadensis* refers to Canada, where elk live as northern climate animals.

The common name "Moose" was coined in the early 1600s and is unique to North America. Worldwide, moose are known as elk—which can be confusing for us since we use that name for our native elk. Our name for moose originated from the Algonquian Indian word *moosu*. It means "one who strips off" and correctly describes the moose's feeding behavior of stripping leaves off stems. The scientific name *Alces alces* means "elk" or "moose."

Elk

Key Deer

VARIETIES ACROSS THE LAND

Varieties of deer occur regionally in North America. In White-tailed Deer, there are 17 subspecies. They range from the tiny Key Deer, which live only in the Florida Keys, to the big boys in northern states, called Dakota Deer. Coues Deer, also called Arizona Deer, are found in Arizona, New Mexico and northern Mexico, while Columbia White-tailed Deer make their homes in the Pacific Northwest.

In many areas, subspecies are difficult to tell apart. Combine that with cross-breeding, which happens at range edges, and it gets even harder to identify them unless they are isolated, like Key Deer.

Mule Deer are the largest deer in the *Odocoileus* genus. They represent about a quarter of all deer in North America, with an estimated 30 million Whitetails and 10 million Mule Deer. Mule Deer are named for their large mule-like ears. They have significantly different antlers and completely different tails than Whitetails. They also differ in how they run. Mule Deer have a bouncy, four-legged spring step that Whitetails lack.

Mule Deer

Elk have four subspecies in North America, with only slight differences in the size and shape of bodies and antlers. Rocky Mountain Elk are the most common and widespread. If you have been to Yellowstone, Grand Teton or Rocky Mountain National Park, you've seen these animals. They are the largest elk, with males obtaining the largest body and antler sizes.

Roosevelt Elk, also known as Olympic Elk, are also large-bodied with impressive antlers. They live in the forests of Washington, Oregon and northern California. Some argue that Roosevelt Elk are the largest subspecies.

Manitoban Elk occur across the Midwest and into Canada. They are thought to have smaller antlers than Rocky Mountain Elk. Not all elk in the Midwest are Manitoban, however. Many individuals in North and South Dakota, for example, were relocated from the Rocky Mountains to help reestablish the decreasing Dakota populations.

Tule Elk, a much smaller subspecies, are scattered in small pockets of California's Central Valley. They are typically about half the size of Rocky Mountain Elk. Except for the Tule, it is extremely difficult to tell elk subspecies apart.

Elk

Moose

There are also four moose subspecies, but each is distinct with a well-defined range. Alaskan Moose make their homes throughout Alaska and into parts of Canada's Yukon. They tend to be the largest and darkest of all moose. Northwestern Moose occur from northwestern Canada to Ontario and down into North Dakota, Minnesota and Michigan. Shiras Moose are seen in the Rocky Mountains in Idaho, Montana, Wyoming and Colorado. Eastern Moose are found in New England and into Canada. The Eastern is the smallest of all moose subspecies.

Moose

White-tailed Deer, white

WAS THAT A WHITE DEER?

In pockets throughout the country you may see a white White-tailed Deer. White Whitetails are actually more common than you might think, but they are still rare and protected in some states. In most cases, they're not albinos. They have blue or brown eyes and dark or pink noses and hooves, and they produce babies with brown, tan or white fur. Their condition, called leucism, is common in nearly all animals, including many bird species.

White-tailed Deer, piebald

Leucistic deer with patches of brown or black are called piebald. Piebald is another mutation and a sign of other issues. Often piebald deer have hunched backs or bowed legs.

On the other end of the spectrum are very dark or nearly black White-tailed Deer. These unusual-looking animals are much more rare than white deer. Their aberration, called melanism, is caused by excessive melanin, the substance that gives deer their normal coloration.

White-tailed Deer, black

TESTAMENT TO BERGMANN'S RULE

Physics asserts that the greater the body mass, the easier it is to retain heat and stay warm. Conversely, the smaller the body mass, the easier it is to lose heat and stay cool. As proof, White-tailed Deer in the northern reaches of their range are the largest, and they get progressively smaller to the south. Whitetail bucks in northern states, such as Minnesota and Wisconsin, can weigh over 200 pounds, while those in the South are usually about 100 pounds. Farther south in the Florida Keys, Key Deer weigh only 50–75 pounds and stand less than 3 feet tall. This overall size variation from north to south is called Bergmann's Rule.

Moose, the largest deer family members, live only in the coldest parts of northern climates. They stand over 7 feet tall at the shoulder, weigh a hefty 700–1,400 pounds and can survive in extreme conditions partly because of their massive size.

Moose

If a deer were to live its life free of predators and human hunters, the limiting factor of its life span would be how long its teeth would last. White-tailed and Mule Deer feed on rough, tough foods, such as twigs, leaves and acorns, which wear down the teeth in about 10–12 years. Few deer in the wild, however, make it to the upper limits of old age. Some live only 3 years due to hunting, vehicle collisions and predators. Others live to reach upwards of 10 years of age. Captive deer can live extended lives of more than 20 years.

Mule Deer

The life span of elk can reach 15–20 years. Most tend to live longer than deer, but their adult years are so considerably shortened by hunters and predators that their population is not significantly increasing.

Moose can live 15–20 years, with the prime of life at 7–12 years. But similar to deer and elk, their life span is greatly reduced due to hunting and other human activities.

Elk

Moose

When the first European settlers came to North America, they found a land teaming with large animals that could provide them with food for long periods. There were 20 million Whitetails at that time, but by the late 1800s, the population plunged to fewer than 500,000 individuals. Mule Deer, which are the western cousins of White-tailed Deer, also declined dramatically. Today in many eastern regions, deer have been reintroduced and are doing well. In some areas the deer population is higher now than at any other time in history.

Historically, there were six elk subspecies in North America. Two subspecies, the native Eastern Elk and Merriam's Elk, were hunted out and have been extinct for more than 100 years. Most folks now living in the eastern half of the United States may not even realize that our Eastern Elk is extinct. Starting in 1913, elk from the Yellowstone region were moved eastward to reintroduce the species. Successful introductions occurred in Arkansas, Tennessee, Kentucky, Wisconsin and the Great Smoky Mountains National Park.

Moose

Moose fared no better and were eliminated from many regions before the elk were exterminated. Since the early 1900s, the remaining population suffered a sharp decrease in numbers. Today there are only 300,000 moose in the United States and just over 500,000 individuals in Canada. Furthermore, in Minnesota the population dropped by three-quarters in fewer than 12 years! If this trend continues, it won't be long before all moose will be gone from the Land of 10,000 Lakes.

Management of our large animals greatly favors White-tailed Deer. Nearly all monies are assigned to increase deer populations for hunters, with little allocated to benefit elk and moose. I believe we are neglecting these larger cousins of deer.

White-tailed Deer

HERDS AND HAREMS

White-tailed Deer live in a matriarchal society, usually led by the oldest
female. The group often consists of only 2–3 generations because females
tend to form their own group once they reach 3 years of age. It's common
to see females fighting and sparring. As long as the leader is in good physical
shape, she can maintain her position of power. If not, a stronger female will
take over, relegating the weaker doe to a lesser role.

Whitetail males also form herds of similar sizes and ages. During the non-breeding season, the bucks move about with the food supply, feeding together. These are called bachelor herds.

White-tailed Deer

Seldom will you see one elk by itself. Elk are known as herd animals. Except during breeding season, cows and bulls live separately in same-sex herds. Cow herds range from six individuals to several hundred. Bull herds have just a few males to upwards of 25, although in some places herds include as many as 50 males. Rarely can a large bull control a breeding harem of more than 24 cows. Many herds of cows are too big for even the largest bull to manage, so the large herds become fractured.

Elk

Moose

Moose

Except for mothers with calves, moose tend to be solitary throughout the year. Cows without calves move about freely and frequently don't associate with other cows—though sometimes they appear to be a herd when they all hang out in an area with good food sources. During the non-breeding season, bull moose usually spend time in small groups of 3–4 individuals. These are often males of a similar age and size. They are congenial toward each other in summer, but this will all change when breeding season rolls around.

Moose

Scientists who study animal behavior have proven that communication among animals of the same species is both complex and comprehensive. Some animals can even communicate with different species! Communication in deer, elk and moose falls into four broad categories: sexual, neonatal, integrative and agonistic.

Sexual communiqués lead to mating activities such as courtship and breeding. Neonatal messages strengthen the bond between mothers and babies. In these conversations, a mother may summon her fawns or instruct a calf to stay put while she goes off to feed.

Moose

Integrative communications convey information about approaching predators and other danger, as well as the location of food. These cooperative exchanges are extremely important in herds and are key to their success.

Agonistic messages deliver threats and challenges that lead to sparring or fighting. It's usually better to settle disputes with vocalizations and body language than to risk getting injured in a fight.

White-tailed Deer

SCENT COMMUNICATION

Communicating with scent is one of the main ways that deer, elk and moose "talk." Odors produced by scent glands on different parts of the body stimulate a wide variety of responses in recipient animals. Scents arouse curiosity, indicate sexual readiness, cause fights and so much more.

Scents may be airborne or deposited on branches, stumps or the ground. A recipient can catch the scent as it floats on the air or smell the location of the deposit.

Scent glands of deer, elk and moose are all over the body—on the forehead; around the eyes (tear duct or preorbital), nose (nasal) and mouth (salivary); between the hind legs near the groin (preputial); on the inside of each hind leg at the ankle (tarsal); on the outside of each hind foot (metatarsal); and between the toes of each foot (interdigital).

LEAVE A NOTE, PLEASE

The forehead glands are active year-round, with increased enlargement and staining in male deer during the mating season, or the rut. The more dominant the buck, the more the forehead swells and becomes darkly stained. The glands are less prominent in females and don't change in size. During the rut, a male will deposit his scent from these glands on prominent places around his home range. Females typically visit these scattered scent posts to "check the mail" from the male.

Tear duct glands, also called preorbital glands, are in a fold of skin in the front corner of each eye. These glands are more prominent in elk, and males use them to show sexual readiness. Male deer, elk and moose in rut use the glands mainly while making a scrape, or signpost, in the ground. Usually this scent is deposited on twigs, sticks and small branches around the scrape. The male closes his eyes and slowly rubs one eye across a stick to leave the scent. When scent marking, the look of satisfaction on his face is remarkable!

White-tailed Deer

38

White-tailed Deer

White-tailed Deer

White-tailed Deer

DROPS OF SCENT

The nose of a deer, elk or moose is normally moist. This is a result of underlying glands that keep the nose damp. Moisture helps trap scent molecules more efficiently, allowing better olfactory function. Animals lick their noses to increase it.

During the rut, the nose is extra moist and often drips. When an animal deposits forehead and tear duct scents, its nasal drippings add extra odor to the scent posts. Anything the nose comes in contact with obtains this distinctive nasal scent.

The tarsal glands, or ankle glands, are on the inside of the ankle joint in each hind leg. Both sexes have these glands, but they are only very active in males during the rut, when they are easily seen as dark, swollen spots. If you get close enough, you can also smell them.

The tarsal glands secrete oil with a unique odor—a different one from that produced during the rut. This changes to a strong, musky odor when an animal urinates and lets the urine drip down its hind legs onto the oil. In addition, animals rub the glands together, concentrating the scent. During the rut, the more dominant the male, the more he urinates and rubs the glands together, resulting in stained hairs. Often these are nearly black, with dark stains running down to the hooves.

The metatarsal glands are on the outside of the hind feet. These are small and virtually inactive in White-tailed Deer. In Mule Deer they are much larger. Most agree that these glands must have been important at one time in the history of deer, but it appears that they are no longer used.

Elk

Moose

SCENTED TRACKS

Between the toes of each foot are the interdigital glands. These aren't normally visible because the animal is standing on them and long hairs cover them. As a deer, elk or moose walks, the long hairs transfer an oily, smelly substance from the glands to the ground—so with each step the animal takes, it is putting down scent! This is the odor that one deer, elk or moose uses to track another. It enables one animal to know the exact steps an individual has taken and track that individual for miles. Males simply follow the scented tracks to find females for breeding.

If you've ever walked in the woods and startled a deer, no doubt you heard a loud snort. White-tailed Deer snort to signal two different alarms. One is a loud snort, given with the mouth shut. Air is so forcefully expelled that it causes the nostrils to flutter, making a distinctive sound.

A Whitetail will make this snort when it senses peril but can't pinpoint it. This alarm warns the herd and also predators that may be nearby, such as wolves and cougars, which rely on the element of surprise. Usually the snorter stands its ground or moves toward the potential danger to flush it out or get closer to smell it. Sometimes it stomps the ground with each step and bobs its head.

In response, the herd stands rigidly, looking and smelling to detect the apparent trouble. If the animals don't perceive danger, they watch the snorter for signs of the next move. Deer won't run before a threat is identified because they might run the wrong way, into a predator. When the snorter is satisfied that the area is safe, the herd relaxes and returns to feeding.

When danger is identified as a real threat, a Whitetail gives a high-pitched, whistle-like snort. A deer makes this sound by forcefully exhaling through its nostrils with its mouth slightly open. While issuing the alarm, the deer turns and runs with tail up and high in the air as a visual signal to the herd that the peril is genuine. All the other deer spring into action and follow in retreat. They raise their tails and wave them back and forth like flags, flashing the white undersides to advertise the alert status as they flee.

White-tailed Deer

Rutting Whitetail bucks create obvious signposts of ground or hoof scrapes in their home ranges. A dominant male chooses a spot on the ground, usually beneath a thin branch hanging just above his head, which will indicate his size. Scraping the ground with his front hooves, he exposes 2–4 feet of soil. With each pass of his hooves, dirt and leaves are thrown up to 10 feet away as he lays down scent from his interdigital glands.

White-tailed Deer

White-tailed Deer

Next, the buck steps into the center of the scrape and urinates, allowing the urine to run down his hind legs and rinse his tarsal glands. Rubbing his legs together, the tarsal glands touch as the urine soaks the earth, leaving a powerful scent.

Now the buck arches his neck and reaches for the low branch over the scrape. He rubs his forehead and tear duct glands on the branch tip. Eventually he grabs the stick with his mouth and bites it, crushing the wood and leaving a salivary scent on it. To increase the scent, he also licks the stick.

Rutting elk and moose make similar signposts. They paw the ground with their front hooves and occasionally use their antlers to break up the newly exposed earth. Like Whitetail bucks, they urinate in the broken soil, but they don't use licking sticks. Instead, elk roll around in the scrape to spread the scent, and moose stomp their feet in the wet mud, splashing it onto their necks and antlers. Some believe that the loose skin hanging from the neck, called the bell or dewlap, collects the scented mud and helps disseminate their scent.

White-tailed Deer

TREE AND SHRUB RUBS

During the rut, most male deer make rubs on small trees for other bucks to see. Using their antlers, they rub and scrape off the soft outer bark, creating conspicuous signposts of reddish or whitish inner bark. Rubs are often made along forest edges, where they are the most noticeable and can be visible from great distances.

Rubs are not just visual signposts. During the process, animals deposit their unique scents from the forehead, tear duct, nasal and salivary glands onto the inner bark. I've often seen rutting bucks nibble at freshly torn bark and lick the new rub to leave a more potent scent.

Males usually make rubs on thin sapling trees, but they also rub thicker trees in the home range. Whitetail rubs help define a buck's home range and communicate details about himself, such as the time of his last visit, his breeding status, size and even his dominancy.

Elk and moose make similar rubs, usually to entire shrubs. They rake their massive antlers over conspicuous shrubs and scent them liberally as signposts.

White-tailed Deer tree rub

51

Elk

Male elk take verbal communication to the next level. Bulls advertise their dominance and sexual readiness with long, high-pitched calls that sound like blasts of a horn, known as bugling. Most bugling occurs during the mating season in autumn, but I have also heard males bugle mournfully in early spring. Elk often finish calling with a series of low, guttural grunts and groans.

Young bulls bugle less heartily than older, larger bulls, which bugle vigorously. Regardless, bugling is dramatic, distinctive and carries across great distances in elk country. A bugling male lets other males know that he owns and is attending the harem in the area.

Elk

MOOSE THAT WOO

Bull moose in rut are much less vocal than bull elk. They only make a low grunt, relying mostly on their noses to detect female scents and roaming far and wide to find cows.

Once a bull locates a female, he makes a scrape, urinates in it, and then kicking at the ground, splashes the urine all over himself. Females are stimulated by the urine scent of bulls and compete with each other to wallow in a soaked scrape. Sometimes they get so excited by the scrape and the urine that they run in circles around the male, bumping him out of the scrape before he is finished.

Moose

FUR COATS

Elk and moose grow one new coat annually, while White-tailed Deer grow two. A deer's summer coat is short in length and bright russet, but the color can be darker or lighter, depending on the place of residence. In moister environments, such as the deciduous forests of the East Coast, deer are dark reddish brown. Deer in the desert Southwest tend to have much lighter coats.

The summer coat is dense and does a good job of reflecting the sun's energy instead of absorbing it, allowing the animals to stay cooler. With very little hair on the ears during summer, body heat dissipates through the ears more easily, which helps to avoid overheating. The normally long guard hairs on the coats are now short, measuring only three-quarters of an inch. A small gland at the base of each hair secretes an oily substance (sebum) that helps waterproof the fur and repels biting insects.

The winter coat starts growing in August and takes three months to complete. These coats range from dark tan to brown to light gray and tend to get lighter in the season as the sun bleaches the fur.

White-tailed Deer

White-tailed Deer

White-tailed Deer

During winter, the coat has about 2,600 guard hairs per square inch. When fully grown, these will be 2–3 inches long. Each hair is hollow and rather coarse and brittle. Guard hairs are mostly for weather protection, to shield the undercoat. The undercoat is a layer of woolly hair that does not allow heat to escape and keeps deer warm in winter. The effect of this dense insulation can be seen during winter storms, when snow accumulates on the coat instead of melting through to the skin.

Elk velvet

ANTLER VELVET

All deer family members grow antlers in the same way. The endocrine system releases a hormone, causing bone salts to deposit on and grow outward from two attachment points on the skull, called pedicles. A network of blood vessels in a layer of modified skin covers the growing antlers and nourishes their growth. The skin-like layer looks and feels like velvet, giving the substance the name.

Velvet has an outer layer of coarse collagen fibers and an inner layer of fine fibers. The blood supply comes from the temporal arteries, with many veins returning the blood to the body. There is also a network of nerves throughout the velvet, allowing the animals to feel their delicate antlers and avoid branches and other objects while on the move.

At the end of summer, when antler growth has reached its maximum, the blood supply to the velvet stops and the skin layer begins to die. The velvet splits, peels and starts to fall off. As it dries, the animal rubs it on shrubs and trees to remove it and eats the long strands, gaining the nutrients. This process can take a half hour to two days.

Moose peeling velvet

White-tailed Deer

DEER ANTLERS

Antlers are curious adornments. They are temporary appendages that grow in all species of the deer family and are lost each year. Only males grow them, except in caribou. Female White-tailed Deer with antlers occur only rarely. Only one doe in 3,000 has an extra amount of the male hormone testosterone in her body, which causes this condition.

Antlers are pure bone, without marrow. Composed of calcium, phosphorous and trace minerals, most of the minerals are obtained from the body; others are supplied by the diet. Calcium is drawn from the male's bones. This can be problematic when it causes a calcium deficiency resulting in temporary osteoporosis.

Antlers grow exceptionally fast, about a quarter inch per day. Generally, most male Whitetails have the largest antlers during ages 5–9, when they are experiencing the prime years of health.

White-tailed Deer

Elk

Bull elk have huge antlers. They start antler growth at 1 year of age, usually in June. At first they grow only 2 thin spikes, but these sometimes fork or split. Spike antlers stay intact until 2 years of age. Slightly older males grow longer, thicker antlers that branch. This growth period is longer, so the antlers get larger, with 3–4 points on each side. At 4–5 years they get the large, classic, multi-tined antlers, which take about 140 days to grow. Antler size maxes out at age 6, after 150 days or so of growth. This is when a large bull can develop antlers that weigh over 40 pounds, extend 5 feet high and have a 5-foot-wide spread! After this time, antler size decreases.

Elk

MOOSE ANTLERS

Bull moose antlers are massive and very heavy, but compared with the animal's total body weight and size, they are only moderately large. In Alaska and northwestern Canada, the largest moose have the largest sets of antlers. Although one record-setting antler weighed nearly 80 pounds, individual antlers can weigh about 50 pounds each! Moose in southern regions have smaller antlers weighing 35 pounds on each side. The best antlers are grown during ages 7–12, with the largest bulls growing the largest antlers in about 150 days.

Bull moose consider antler size in their decisions to fight for breeding dominance. I once observed this in an unusual way in Canada with eminent moose researcher Vince Crichton. After strapping on a stuffed, antlered moose head, Vince would approach another bull. If the live male had smaller antlers, it would retreat. When its antlers were larger or the same size, it became agitated, indicating a challenge and a willingness to fight. Standing just a foot away, I have never been more uncomfortable taking photographs of moose!

Moose

ANTLER SHEDS

When food is least abundant during December and January, testosterone levels decrease in males, causing adhesion of the antlers to loosen. Males must feel this because they shake their heads violently from side to side to rid themselves of the adornments. Often one antler falls off, leaving a patch of reddish skin and a few beads of blood. Usually within 24 hours the second antler drops.

Most shedding occurs in January and February. In White-tailed Deer, elk and moose, it usually starts with the smallest, least dominant males. In one locality I observed large, dominant male Whitetails carry their antlers into April before shedding, but in Yellowstone in late February, the biggest elk still had antlers. When antlers drop late, a new set starts growing shortly thereafter. Late sheds aren't common in all deer populations or in elk and moose.

White-tailed Deer

During midwinter, it's become a popular sport to look for antler sheds. The challenge is to find a matching pair. Dogs are trained to find sheds just like hunting dogs are trained to find upland birds. Regardless, nothing in nature is wasted. Mice and other small rodents gnaw on antlers that people have not picked up. Gnawing wears down their ever-growing teeth, and they benefit from the rich source of calcium. To determine how long it would take for a large deer antler to be consumed, I once wired one to a post. Before two years passed, the antler was gnawed down to a nubbin.

White-tailed Deer antler

White-tailed Deer

There are big differences between antlers and horns. Horns are permanent structures that are never shed. When they break off during a fight, they don't grow back. Mountain goats, bison, bighorn sheep and other hoofed animals have horns. In the species with horns, usually both sexes have them, with larger horns adorning the males.

Horns have a porous core of bone covered with a layer of keratin—the same protein that makes up your fingernails and hair. Horns are nourished by internal blood flow. This is unlike antlers, which have an external blood flow when velvet covers them. Growing continuously throughout an animal's life, horns become larger or longer with each passing year. Many show annual growth rings, indicating the animal's age.

Many folks confuse antlers with horns because they resemble each other, but you can appreciate the distinctions by knowing the facts. These are always worth learning to get it right.

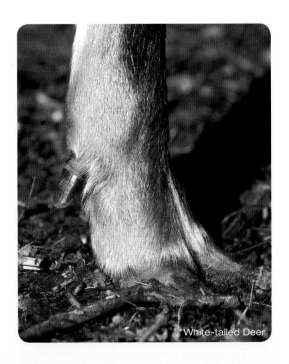
White-tailed Deer

TOES IN HOOVES

Hooves are a fascinating feature of deer, elk and moose. They function as durable footwear that keeps the feet dry, provides traction and performs well in most weather. They also facilitate self-defense.

Deer, elk and moose have four toes on each foot. Two toes, called dewclaws, don't normally touch the ground because they're located high on the foot. The animals walk on their other two toes, like ballerinas on tiptoes. The tips of these toes are encased in keratin—a strong protein that makes up the hooves. Like our fingernails, deer hooves continually grow, averaging an eighth of an inch per week. Normal walking and running keeps this growth in check.

Moose

White-tailed Deer

SURE-FOOTED TREAD

Each hoof has a hard outer casing that provides for great footing in soil or on rock. The center of the hoof, called the frog (subunguinis), is spongy or fleshy and protrudes slightly. The frog gives extra traction on wet and slippery surfaces, but it recedes into the hard outer casing during winter. This makes it difficult for deer, elk and moose to walk on frozen lakes and other icy surfaces, and it is why you may see them sprawling on ice with legs in all directions. They need to get off the ice somehow before they can get up and walk.

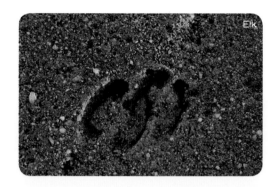
Elk

The front legs and hooves of deer, elk and moose are longer and larger than their hind legs. Most of the weight is in the front half of the body, and the larger legs and hooves help support it. So when you see tracks in mud or sand, it's often possible to identify the front print from the back by the depth of the impression. Front hooves are also pointed and the two toes angle toward each other, helping to identify the direction of travel.

Range and track size can help you distinguish deer tracks from those of elk and moose. Deer leave tracks that are 2–3 inches long and 1½–2 inches wide, while elk tracks are 4–5 inches long and 3 inches wide. Moose tracks, at 5–6 inches long and 4 inches wide, are significantly larger than those of deer.

Moose

A GREAT OLFACTORY SYSTEM

When a deer licks its nose, the tongue suddenly flicks out, slaps against the nostrils and returns into the mouth. Deer, elk and moose do this to gain information from the environment. With each lick, the animal wets the part of the nose that traps incoming scents and refreshes it to gather new smells.

Deer have the incredible ability to smell even the slightest odor from afar. Ask hunters who have tried hard to cover their human scent—deer can still smell them well before seeing them. Under ideal conditions, with air temperature at 60–70 °F, humidity at 50–70 percent and a slight breeze, deer and elk can detect human scent from a half mile away or more!

White-tailed Deer

Elk

Moose

Moose

EARS TO HEAR

The ability to hear from long distances is almost as important as the sense of smell. White-tailed Deer ears are about 7 inches long and 4 inches wide. Mule Deer ears are much larger, about 9 inches long and 6½ inches wide. Elk and moose have very large ears as well. Their large ears act like satellite dishes, collecting even the slightest of sounds.

Pivoting the ears in all directions and independently provides a great range of hearing. Often they point one ear in one direction and the other the opposite way. Switching positions back and forth, they make slight adjustments to pinpoint the source of sounds.

Deer, elk and moose also hear in extremely high frequencies, like dogs. In fact, if you blow a dog whistle—which makes sounds we can't hear—these animals will turn to hear it.

White-tailed Deer

Keeping an alert eye on the surroundings is the key to survival, and deer, elk and moose do this with outstanding vision. Not only can they see predators approaching from far away, they have no trouble seeing midrange and up close as they forage for food.

The eye position on the sides of the head enables a wide field of view. In humans the range is about 170–180 degrees. It's much greater in deer, elk and moose, about 300–310 degrees. These animals can see nearly all around them except for directly behind.

Moose

The eyes are usually brown, with large rectangular pupils. The rectangular shape lets in more light, allowing for better vision in low light. The animals are crepuscular, meaning they are most active in early morning and at twilight, when light is diminished. Unlike humans, they lack a yellow filter in their lenses, permitting them to see in the blue range of light better—a tremendous help in low light. It is estimated that they can see upwards of 1,000 times better than people can in weak light.

Deer, elk and moose have dichromatic vision. This means they can see violet, blue, green and yellow regions of light. They cannot see red and orange colors, which is why hunters wear blaze orange during hunting season.

White-tailed Deer

White-tailed Deer

EYESHINE

In darkness, the eyes of these animals shine white
to silver when they meet with a flashlight beam or
headlights. This is caused by a mirror-like surface at
the back of each retina, called the tapetum lucidum,
or bright curtain. When light enters their eyes, rods
and cones pick up the initial flood of light. Light
that escapes the rods and cones reflects off the tapeta
lucida, giving both eyes a second chance to gather
light and making them efficient at utilizing all of the
available light. We lack this feature, which is why
red-eye reflecting the blood vessels in our eyes shows
in our photos taken with a flash.

White-tailed Deer

CUTTING-EDGE BITE

Whitetails have 32 teeth—the same number as adult humans. However, deer, elk and moose lack upper incisors. They have a bony plate instead that makes them bite into food differently.

When we eat an apple, we cut off a piece with our upper and lower teeth. Deer, elk and moose bite into twigs with their bottom incisors and tear off the rest. To know what critter is eating your shrubs, look at a chewed-off stem. If it has a clean, sharp cut, the culprit is a rabbit or rodent. If only half the stem is neatly cut and there are curled strands of torn wood fiber, it is a deer, elk or moose.

Elk

Moose

89

Moose

Elk

White-tailed Deer

AMBLING TO FULL SPEED

Deer, elk and moose share the same type of gait. The front right leg moves at the same time as the rear left and alternates with the opposite combination. They walk at about 3–4 mph, which is faster than people generally walk. Trotting moves them up to around 6–10 mph and can be sustained for a fairly long time. Running White-tailed Deer have been clocked at 20–25 mph, but they can accelerate to nearly 40 mph for short distances.

To evade predators, White-tailed Deer employ a simple but effective strategy of bolting quickly and running fast—so fast that they often outrun the danger. They can maintain this high speed for fairly long distances, something most predators can't do.

Elk are extremely fast runners and easily match the speeds of deer. Bulls can run short bursts at upwards of 45 mph, and cows and calves can maintain high speeds for longer distances. I've watched elk run at high speeds up a mountainside that I just had difficulty climbing.

I once watched a wolf chase an elk cow. She ran full speed down a mountainside in snow 3 feet deep and continued to run at high speed with the wolf in pursuit for over 2 miles. Eventually she made it to a river and ran right into the icy water, chest deep. The wolf had no choice but to give up. Her speed and sure-footedness kept her alive, and it was exciting to watch.

Moose have the capability to run fast but often don't due to their massive size. Although known for their ambling slow nature, if they want to move, they will do so quickly. Their long legs enable them to run short distances at 30–35 mph.

Elk

Mule Deer

STOTTING ESCAPES

Mule Deer escape predators differently. Living in steep, rocky habitats, they bound or spring away in a distinctive bouncing run called a stot. Using all four legs simultaneously, they spring up, quickly ascending ridges and jumping over boulders and other obstacles that predators find impossible to follow. You can always positively identify a Mule Deer when it stots.

A bounding animal will push forcefully with its hind legs, sending itself upward and forward while tucking its front legs underneath. Just before coming to ground, the front legs extend and land together, supporting the entire body weight. The hind legs land next, just forward of the front legs. So when you see bounding tracks, the front tracks will be imprinted (registered) just behind the rear hoof prints. Sets of tracks may be far apart, since White-tailed Deer can leap about 30 feet!

White-tailed Deer

White-tailed Deer

JUMPING ABILITIES

White-tailed Deer can easily jump over a 6-foot fence without much effort. I've seen foraging deer suddenly spring over a 5-foot fence and continue eating as if nothing happened. It is thought that deer can clear a 9-foot fence, and I don't question it.

Deer can also jump long distances horizontally, up to 29 feet to the side! Jumping sideways is quite possibly one of their best survival tactics. When being chased by predators, the ability to run fast and jump any which way is critical for staying alive.

Elk are also good at jumping. An adult elk can jump as high as 15 feet in a single bound! Moose are not big jumpers because of their size, but they possess the ability as well and will jump to dodge predators or other danger.

White-tailed Deer

White-tailed Deer

White-tailed Deer

GAME TRAILS

When startled or pursued by a predator, deer, elk and moose quickly run and usually head for some kind of cover, such as the forest. If not pursued, they often stop at the edge of woods and look back.

However, when deer are just moving from one place to another, such as from a bedding spot to a feeding area, they nearly always use established game trails. Usually these trails have been in use for generations. They often wind through deep cover, follow gentle slopes and avoid major obstacles.

In the mountains, elk travel from high country to the lowlands via generational pathways. Moose tend to follow the same paths through forests and willow thickets, creating a network of game trails.

White-tailed Deer

Moose

SWIMMING

Water is a safe haven for deer, elk and moose. Deer are excellent swimmers and will swim across rivers and lakes to move from one area to another. Elk are also good swimmers and often use their ability to escape predators. Moose can swim up to 6 miles an hour for long periods and dive down to 17 feet to feed on the bottom of ponds. They spend a lot of time in the water, retreating from the hot sun and biting insects. Moose babies start swimming at about 7 days of age.

White-tailed and Mule Deer are selective feeders and can be extremely particular about the types of plants they eat, depending on the season. They have narrow muzzles that enable them to nibble on their choice of twigs, leaves, berries, flowers and bark while avoiding other plants.

Elk have larger muzzles and graze on grasses and low-growing plants in mountainous habitats. In spring they also eat a variety of tender shoots of sedge, and twigs from a wide range of shrubs later in the season.

The huge muzzles and lips of moose limit grazing to large clumps of grasses and other obvious food sources. Like the deer and elk menu, season dictates the moose diet. They eat a more limited variety of food than deer and elk, feeding on plants in water if available in spring. Their main diet is willow, and they nimbly strip hundreds of leaves in minutes from branches, leaving just the twigs from spring through fall. In winter they eat the willow twigs and bark.

Moose

CREPUSCULAR DINING

Deer, elk and moose just grab and swallow food by the mouthful. They move about mainly at dusk and dawn (crepuscular), gathering and swallowing large quantities without much chewing. Some feeding occurs at night (nocturnal).

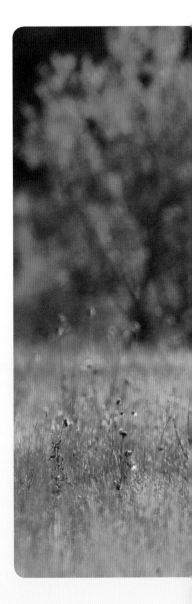

Elk

CHEWING THE CUD

Deer family members are ruminants with large four-chambered stomachs. The first chamber, called the rumen, holds the swallowed food that wasn't chewed and partially digests it. Moose have smaller rumens than deer and elk because the willow leaves they eat are low in fiber, high in nutrition and easy to digest. The other three chambers are digestive compartments that work to complete the break-down of food.

Sometime after swallowing food, the animal sits and regurgitates the partly digested food, or cud, back into the mouth. Slowly it chews the cud, which helps break it down further. If you get a chance to watch this activity, you would see a large mass of food, called a bolus, the size of a golf or tennis ball moving up the neck and into the mouth. When the animal finishes chewing, the item is swallowed again for additional digestion. Due to the diet, deer and elk need to chew the cud more than moose.

White-tailed Deer, white

Moose

These animals tend to concentrate their feeding on plants that are in abundance and at peak freshness. They have remarkable memories for good sources of food. I have seen White-tailed Deer return to the same spot each year to feed for a week. Studies show that all deer family members choose the most nutritional plants available during the season. This behavior is not based on taste but is perhaps learned from their mothers.

In spring the animals consume foods that tend to be high in vitamins and plant protein, such as herbs and grasses. At this time males are starting to grow antlers, so they need to feed heavily on these emerging plants. Feeding decreases dramatically during summer due to daytime heat. By mid to late August, food intake begins to shift into high gear, called hyperphagia.

BULKING UP

During hyperphagia, deer, elk and moose feed heavily to gain as much body fat as possible for winter. Males are also bulking up for breeding season, when they will hardly eat at all. By late summer, deer look for oak, hickory and beech trees and feed heavily on acorns and other nuts. In some years nuts comprise upwards of 80 percent of the diet. Deer put on more fat from acorns than any other food source, with Whitetails consuming up to 9 pounds of food per day.

White-tailed Deer

Elk

Elk and also moose require so much food that when they're not resting, they're eating. It is estimated that a large bull elk needs 3–5 pounds of food per day for every 100 pounds of body weight just to maintain its health. Depending on body size, a male elk can require as much as 55 pounds of vegetation per day! Males need the highest quality food and lots of it during antler development, and nursing females require additional food to supplement milk production. One study reported elk feeding for more than 13 hours a day.

Feeding behavior changes dramatically during winter. After frost kills the herbaceous plants, the animals eat dried grasses. When snow reaches a foot deep or more, they browse for twigs. Small twigs at the end of last year's growth, often half the diameter of a pencil, are now the preferred food. The oldest twigs have the least nutritional content, and new bark on twigs provides the most nourishment. Some have estimated that a 150-pound White-tailed Deer requires 8–10 pounds of twigs daily to survive, or 10,000–13,000 twig tips per day.

Willow bark has lots of nutrition, but it's also highly toxic. For moose, this isn't a problem because they have an exceptionally large liver that metabolizes toxic plant compounds. Actually, their specialized willow diet reduces the competition for food and is an advantage for them during winter.

Elk

SALTY PREFERENCE

Aquatic plants are high in protein and especially sodium. Sodium is absent in many plants, and moose like to feed on sodium-rich aquatic plants after a long, hard winter. I traveled throughout North America to photograph for this book, and Algonquin Provincial Park in Canada was one of the best places to watch moose feeding on aquatic plants in spring. Alaska is another good place to see them feeding in water.

Moose

Moose

Moose are so extremely tall that it makes feeding
in water and drinking a challenge. To reach their
dinner and drink the water they sometimes kneel to
make it more comfortable.

White-tailed Deer

THE AUTUMN RUT

All members of the deer family mate during a set time each fall. This period, known as the rut, is when males compete for the right to mate and pass on their genes. In most places, White-tailed and Mule Deer breed in October and November. Elk and moose, which live in higher elevations or in areas where winter comes early, mate from late August through November.

Nearly all females are bred during the short time they are ovulating. Females that are not fertilized during the initial mating will return to estrus and be ready to mate again in about 3 weeks. Males stay in breeding condition during the interim and pursue these females again once they are ready.

Moose

117

SPARRING PRACTICE

Sparring equips males with valuable practice and experience for the severe fights to come during the breeding season. In northern areas, Whitetail sparring begins in September and lasts for several months. Elk and moose have a similar time span but start slightly earlier. Sparring becomes more frequent as the breeding season progresses.

White-tailed Deer

Moose

Larger, dominant males teach smaller, younger males the finer points of sparring, so it is common for matches to occur between two males of unequal size or stature. They rub their antlers together to start a match and build muscles in their necks while the inexperienced opponent learns about fighting skills and balance. Sparring also establishes the pecking order among all the males, often preventing actual fights later.

Elk

Fighting is a serious event, often resulting in life-threatening injuries and death. Challenging and fighting occurs only between dominant males of equal size.

White-tail fights are like heavyweight shoving matches. Each buck digs in and starts to push. The larger, heavier and more skillful male wins by throwing his opponent off balance and chasing it away. Rarely the opponent's antler detaches and entangles in the winner's antlers like a trophy.

Elk bulls chase each other first and then stand broadside so the opponent can see their size and antler length. With stiff legs, they make their approach. Lowering their heads, they lock antlers and engage in lethal shoving.

Bull moose don't fight as much as deer and elk. Two individuals walk slowly and deliberately toward each other, rocking their heads back and forth and tilting their antlers from side to side so the other male can get a good look. Judging the size of the opposing antlers to the inch, the male with smaller antlers backs down.

Be sure to respect the space of all large wild animals and do not approach them, especially while their hormones are raging during the rut.

White-tailed Deer

TIME TO MATE

Mating depends on the readiness of the female, and breeding is triggered by the photoperiod. Photoperiod is the amount of daylight from dawn until dusk. Unlike weather patterns that change irregularly in different latitudes, sunrise and sunset consistently signal the start of the breeding season. The photoperiod causes the release of a hormone that prompts the pituitary gland to discharge luteinizing hormones. These cause the female to ovulate and bring her into estrus, making fertilization possible. This period lasts just a short time, often a few days to a week.

About 24–48 hours before ovulation, the female wanders around, holding her tail horizontally and urinating frequently. Pheromones are deposited with the urine, and any passing male picks up the scent that she's ready for breeding. The male stops to smell the urine spots, lifts his head, curls his upper lip and waits. This behavior is called flehmening. The male follows the female until she accepts his advances and copulation occurs.

White-tailed Deer

Moose

Elk

Elk

123

Moose

The dominant male will become the breeder, and he must keep all other males away. Normally there isn't much competition since the pecking order has already been established. However, big fights will break out if a new male shows up.

A bull moose attends only a single cow at a time, even though two or three females may be stimulated simultaneously by his scent. The bull follows his chosen female for a couple days or more, waiting for her to become ready to mate. Once she is bred, he leaves to find another cow and start the process all over again.

White-tailed Deer

Elk

In White-tailed and Mule Deer, the time between conception and birth is just short of 7 months, or 190–210 days. Elk gestate for about 9 months, around 255–270 days. Gestation in moose lasts about 8 months, or 230–240 days. Even though moose are larger than elk, they carry their unborn in the womb for a shorter time and produce smaller babies. If development took longer, it's possible that the babies might grow too large for the smaller mothers to carry.

Moose

Moose

LITTERS OF TWINS

Often the overall health of the mother dictates how many babies she will birth in spring. During the first few years of reproduction, deer and elk mothers give birth to just one baby. In older, more mature females, twins are the norm, and the healthiest of females may even have triplets. Moose generally give birth to one calf, but they can also produce twins.

Despite the birthing of twins or triplets, mothers often have only one baby in tow. The rigors of life, especially in the first few hours and days, are extremely difficult for babies. Black Bears, Grizzly Bears and other predators take many young deer, elk and even moose. Cold, wet weather and separation from the mother also reduce the number of young. In addition, river crossings and other natural obstacles cause the premature death of young elk and moose.

Moose

DELIVERY INTO THE WILD

As birth draws near, female deer and elk withdraw from their herds to a birthing territory. A pregnant moose will also move to a secluded place when it is time to give birth.

About 48 hours before birth, the udder swells with milk. The female experiences labor pains, evidenced by a series of moans and groans. The mother stands just before giving birth, allowing the weight of the baby to pull it down and out of the birth canal. The baby drops to the ground, tearing the placental sac and umbilical cord. Impact with the ground probably helps stimulate its first breath. When twins are delivered, the second sibling is usually born 15–20 minutes after the first.

Mule Deer

White-tailed Deer

NEWBORNS

Immediately the mother begins to lick her newborn to remove any remaining placental sac and clean up blood that might attract a predator. Licking also dries the baby and stimulates it to move around. Often it's a struggle for the baby to stand. Its legs are longer than its body, and the baby needs to coordinate all four legs at once. After it stands, the mother's vigorous licking knocks it over, forcing the baby to try again.

Most try to walk after only 10 minutes, and nearly all are awkwardly successful after 20 minutes. Walking with ease in an hour, babies are running during their first day. At about 5 days of age, they can outrun adult humans.

The first few days of life are the most critical for newly born deer, elk and moose. During this time, babies are kept separate from their siblings. Usually at about 5–6 days of age, they follow the mother and join their littermates.

In many parts of the West, newborn elk are the food staple for wolves and hungry bears just out of hibernation. Whitetail fawns and elk calves have over 200 white spots on their tan coats. The spotting resembles dappled sunlight and helps conceal them, but the main defense is to lay motionless. When this fails, mother deer fend off small predators, and elk and moose actively fight for their calves. Using their front hooves, they try to stomp on the predator. I've seen one mother elk take this further, chasing away a lone wolf in Yellowstone National Park.

Elk

White-tailed Deer

Elk

In the first week or so of life, mother deer and elk seek and join the young about 3–4 times a day. A Whitetail doe gives a soft call, summoning her fawns out of their hiding place. They run to their mother and nurse for 5–10 minutes, ingesting about 6–8 ounces of milk. As they age, milk consumption increases to 12 ounces. Elk follow the same pattern, with calves consuming slightly more milk.

The milk of deer and elk contains about 10 percent butterfat, and moose milk has an even higher fat content. All are more than three times as rich as cow's milk, which has only 3 percent butterfat.

Moose

Unlike deer and elk, moose stick closer to their babies between feedings, and the young grow extremely fast on their rich milk diet. Weighing around 30–35 pounds at birth, they can gain as much as 2–3 pounds per day and grow to at least 300 pounds in just 5 months. While photographing moose for this book, however, I was surprised to see a calf less than one month of age feeding heavily on willow leaves, just like its mother! Although the calf would attempt to feed whenever it could, the mother would allow nursing only about 1–2 times every couple hours.

White-tailed Deer

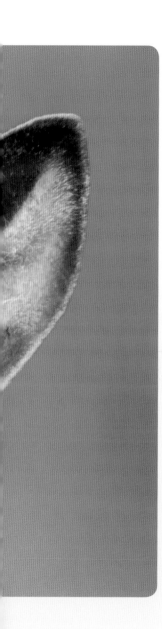

GROWING INTO MATURITY

Young male White-tailed Deer grow antlers in the first few months of life. By the end of their first summer, they may have tiny spikes. They are sexually mature at this time, but the other bucks won't allow them to breed until they are 3–4 years of age, when they are larger. Young female Whitetails become sexually mature at one year. Depending on the dynamics and temperament of their female herd, young does are bred now or later.

ENJOYING OUR DEER, ELK AND MOOSE

We are so fortunate to live with White-tailed Deer in nearly all habitats. People feed them in their backyards and enjoy watching them feed in public parks during the evening. It's a popular pastime.

Folks from around the world come to visit our national parks to see elk. There's hardly anything more magnificent in the fall than a bull elk tending his harem while his bugles echo down the valley.

Moose are some of the most amazing animals. Massive yet genteel in nature, I am in awe each time I photograph them. Whether it's a bull moose on the Alaskan tundra or a tiny baby in the Colorado mountains, the sight of these animals never fails to touch me deeply.

We need to manage deer, elk and moose correctly so they can survive and thrive. There is immense value in seeing them in their natural habitats, and they deserve our best intentions. By educating ourselves, we can make the right choices to ensure that our children and grandchildren will see and enjoy these majestic creatures as we do now.

White-tailed Deer

Elk

Moose

141

This photo spread shows our native deer, elk and moose species in the United States and Canada and their ranges. Ranges in dark red indicate where you would most likely see the animals during the year. Former ranges are shown in tan. Like other wildlife, these animals move around freely and can be seen at different times of the year both inside and outside their ranges. Maps do not indicate the number of individuals in a given area (density).

White-tailed Deer

WHITE-TAILED DEER

MULE DEER

ELK

MOOSE

ABOUT THE AUTHOR

Naturalist, wildlife photographer and writer Stan Tekiela is the originator of the popular nature appreciation book series that includes loons, eagles, bluebirds, owls, hummingbirds, woodpeckers, wolves, bears and deer. For about three decades, Stan has authored more than 120 field guides and wildlife audio CDs for nearly every state in the nation, presenting many species of birds, mammals, reptiles and amphibians, trees, wildflowers and cacti. Holding a Bachelor of Science degree in Natural History from the University of Minnesota and as an active professional naturalist for more than 25 years, Stan studies and photographs wildlife throughout the United States and has received various national and regional awards for his books and photographs. Also a well-known columnist and radio personality, his syndicated column appears in more than 25 newspapers and his wildlife programs are broadcast on a number of Midwest radio stations. Stan can be followed on Facebook and also Twitter. He can be contacted via his web page at www.naturesmart.com.